Making a Rainbow

my science fun

I0884231

Published in the United States of America by Cherry Lake Publishing
Ann Arbor, Michigan
www.cherrylakepublishing.com

Reading Adviser: Marla Conn MS, Ed., Literacy specialist, Read-Ability, Inc.
Book Design: Jennifer Wahl
Illustrator: Jeff Bane

Copyright ©2018 by Cherry Lake Publishing
All rights reserved. No part of this book may be reproduced or utilized in
any form or by any means without written permission from the publisher.

Library of Congress Cataloging-in-Publication Data has been filed and is available at catalog.loc.gov

Printed in the United States of America
Corporate Graphics

About the illustrator: Jeff Bane and his two business partners own a studio along the American River in Folsom, California, home of the 1849 Gold Rush. When Jeff's not sketching or illustrating for clients, he's either swimming or kayaking in the river to relax.

table of contents

Science Notes

Making a Rainbow explores how water can refract light. In this experiment, the reader sprays a garden hose on a sunny day and observes how a rainbow appears. The water separates the beams of light into their different wavelengths, showing up as different colors.

Have you seen a **rainbow**?

A rainbow needs sunlight and water.

When was the last time
you saw a rainbow?

Can you make a rainbow?

Let's find out!

- Yard or garden
- Garden hose
- A sunny day

You will need these things

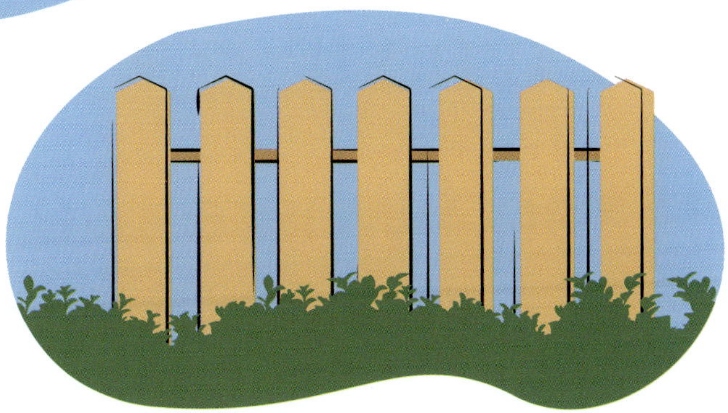

Go outside in your yard or garden.

Turn on the garden hose **faucet**.

Stand where the sun is behind you.

Find the end of the hose.

Put your thumb over it.
The water will spray out.

Is the water warm or cold?

Hold the hose in front of you.
Turn around slowly.

A rainbow will appear in the water.

Why do you think it's so small?

Water makes sunlight separate into different colors.

Try it with a **sprinkler**.

Try it on a cloudy day!

Good job. You're done!
Science is fun!

What new questions do you have?

glossary & index

glossary

faucet (FAW-sit) a tool that water flows out of

rainbow (RAYN-boh) a bend of different colors, caused by the sunlight changing directions as it shines through water mist

sprinkler (SPRING-klur) a device that attaches to a hose and sprays water over a lawn or garden

index